# A MARKET-LED ALTERNATIVE FOR THE CURRICULUM: BREAKING THE CODE

THE LONDON FILE - PAPERS FROM THE
INSTITUTE OF EDUCATION
*Titles in the series include:*

# THE LONDON FILE
### PAPERS FROM THE INSTITUTE OF EDUCATION

# A MARKET-LED ALTERNATIVE FOR THE CURRICULUM: BREAKING THE CODE

## JAMES TOOLEY

INSTITUTE OF
EDUCATION
UNIVERSITY OF LONDON

Published by

the Tufnell Press

PUBLISHED
*by*
**the Tufnell Press**
47, Dalmeny Road, London, N7 0DY





First published 1993

BRITISH LIBRARY CATALOGUING-IN-PUBLICATION DATA
A catalogue record for this book is available from the British Library

ISBN 1 872767 51 6

Book design by Fiona Barlow, Carter Wong, London
Printed in Great Britain by Da Costa Print, London

# CONTENTS

## ACKNOWLEDGEMENTS

Earlier drafts of this work were given to the Durham University branch of the Philosophy of Education Society of Great Britain, and to the Philosophy of Education research seminar at the Institute of Education, University of London. I wish to thank all participants for helpful comments, especially Professor Kevin Harris, Professor Paul H. Hirst, Professor John White, Graham Haydon, Richard Smith, and Patricia White. Financial support was received from the Economic and Social Research Council, under a research studentship competition award.

# TOWARDS MARKET-LED CURRICULA

The National Curriculum is a national disaster. It diverts huge resources away from areas of acute need. It squanders de-professionalised teachers' time in superfluous bureaucracy. It entrusts immense and dangerous powers in the current Secretary of State for Education, of whatever political persuasion. But I do not suppose I am the first to utter these thoughts; and this is not yet another publication against *the* National Curriculum. There are enough of those already. They criticise the current curriculum but stress that it is at fault because 'it's a Tory curriculum', or that it was introduced by a Prime Minister impatient to stamp her authority on wayward schools. These publications are not against national curricula *per se*. Indeed, they usually advance alternative compulsory curricula: leaner, fitter, more democratic, more egalitarian, more politically correct.

This monograph is different—it is a polemic against the very notion of a national curriculum, any national curriculum. But more than that, it is a defence of entrusting curricula to the market. Any mention of the market, and many educationalists get hot under the collar. I think their anxiety is misplaced. My case is that a market-led curriculum would be liberating, empowering and facilitate egalitarian ideals far better than any bureaucratized, centralized curriculum. That is why this present government, despite its rhetoric about the market, holds the National Curriculum as the centrepiece of its reforms. It does not entrust 'power to the people'. That is why the mandarins in their revamped Department for Education have always wanted a national curriculum. The last thing they seek is people empowerment.

Is it foolish to mount this challenge now? At a recent conference, the Chief Executive of the National Curriculum Council reminded his antagonistic audience of the complete consensus behind the principle of a national curriculum. No arguing with him. The principle is accepted by all the major political parties. A comfortable majority of educationalists seem similarly compliant. Why waste effort in a vain attempt to challenge that consensus? It is not only that I am dismayed at the easy acquiescence of educationalists and politicians in this vast expansion of state control of education, and want a dissenting voice to rock their complacency. Nor just that I see the fledgling states of Eastern Europe and the old Soviet Union observing our reforms, and want them to know that these do not necessarily reflect the liberal ideas they are attempting to espouse. Deep down I hope that the debate over national curricula will be reopened. My first hope is that, as I write, the Labour Party is indulging in a rethink of its policies (again). Perhaps they will be open to suggestion? But the Institute for Public Policy Research (IPPR) is waiting in the wings, ready to take up its rightful position of influence, just as the right-wing think tanks did in the Thatcher years. The IPPR has already published its own national curriculum proposals. At least, then, I can point out the flaws in these. A major part of this paper will address the IPPR's work for this reason. Crucially, I want to question the wisdom of diffusing resources throughout the whole community, ostensibly for purposes of equity, when there are pockets of great need which really could do with some targeted help.

My second hope is that, as the National Curriculum begins to buckle under its own weight, opposition from teachers will increase. Perhaps my arguments can speak for those teachers who feel their autonomy and professionalism undermined. Those teachers of seven-year olds whose professional intuition points to the need for more time devoted to reading and basic numeracy, coerced by experts instead to cram their curriculum with 'Blue Peter' technology and meandering investigations; those teachers of eleven-year olds struggling to make sense of the internal contradictions of the mathematics attainment targets; those teachers of history compelled to redefine history as ending 25 years ago; all teachers whose time for their vocation is increasingly taken up by facile form filling to placate bureaucrats. There must be no assumption that things would be better if only some other party had got hold of the curriculum: my argument is that things would be as bad, if not worse.

My third vague hope is that at least I can take part in the debate now beginning over the desirability of a common curriculum for Europe (McLean, 1990). Just an opening salvo at that now, to be taken up more vigorously if and when the debate becomes more serious.

But perhaps my greatest hope is that provided by a little noticed clause in the Education Reform Act. Clause 16 reads:

'For the purposes of enabling development work or experiments to be carried out, the Secretary of State may direct as respects a particular maintained school that, for such a period as may be specified in the direction, the provisions of the National Curriculum (a) shall not apply or (b) shall apply with such modifications as may be so specified.'

Or in plain English, with the Secretary of State's permission, *any school may opt put of the National Curriculum*, in part or in whole. All that a school needs is an application to the Secretary of State from its governing body, with the agreement of the LEA. (Grant-maintained schools only have to have agreement from the governing body). Now that is a mass opt-out that I think many teachers could support. I hope that my writing here will help quell any misgivings that they might have regarding doing this.

So: I set out to challenge the consensus of state-controlled curricula and to present the case for a market-led alternative.

## THE CASE FOR A NATIONAL CURRICULUM: FAILURES OF STATE EDUCATION

The case for a national curriculum has been made both *negatively*, arising out of dissatisfaction with state education in England and Wales, and *positively*, from more philosophical concerns. The dissatisfaction with state education can be traced back to the first of the Black Papers (Cox and Dyson, 1969), through to the 1975 public furore around the William Tyndale Primary School in the London Borough of Islington. The 1976 Ruskin College speech of Labour Prime Minister James Callaghan provoked the 'Great Debate' that laid the foundations for a compulsory core curriculum. This was finally brought to fruition in the 1988 Education Reform Act. The philosophical arguments can usefully be traced back to John White's 1973 *Towards a Compulsory Curriculum*, through to his recent 1990 *Education and the Good Life*.

This chapter focuses on the *negative* arguments: the problems of standards in state schools, lack of equality of opportunity, continuity between primary and secondary schools, 'sink' schools and 'problem' schools, and economic competitiveness. The *positive* philosophical arguments are addressed in the next section: these look at education in, and for, democracy; education for autonomy; and considerations of the nature of knowledge. The IPPR's case is concerned, to lesser or greater extent, with all of these arguments except the last.

## Standards

Low standards in state schools were presented by the Government as an important motivation for introducing its National Curriculum (DES and WO, 1987 pp. 3-4). The IPPR too insists that standards could be raised with the introduction of its curriculum (O'Hear and White, 1991 p. 5).

One area of concern about standards is basic levels of literacy and numeracy. The other concern relates to subjects deemed useful to economic competitiveness—mathematics, science and perhaps technology. The Government argued that their National Curriculum could raise standards in three main ways, through the broadening of the curriculum, setting clear objectives, and ensuring that a 'good' curriculum reaches all. The first two issues will be looked at here, the third will be discussed under 'equality of opportunity'.

### Raising standards 1: broadening the curriculum

Standards can be raised by 'ensuring that all pupils study a broad and balanced range of subjects throughout their compulsory schooling and do not drop too early studies which may stand them in good stead later' (DES and WO, 1987 pp. 3-4). The IPPR's curriculum seems similarly 'broad and balanced', so perhaps this is one way in which they think it, too, might raise standards.

Now it is clear that this 'broadening of the curriculum' cannot be designed to raise standards in literacy and numeracy. It is already claimed that the demand for broadening the curriculum is leading to lower standards in these basic skills: teachers report that basic literacy and numeracy are being crowded out of the curriculum (NCC, 1991 pp. 52 and 64)! A recent survey gave this as a plausible reason for declining reading standards (Cato and Whetton, 1991 p. 67). Presumably, then, the broadening of the curriculum argument relates to the second concern, economic competitiveness. By not allowing some pupils to drop maths and science too early, it is claimed, standards in these areas will be raised.

However, pupils drop these subjects because of lack of motivation, or lack of achievement, or both. Could a simple government injunction coercing these children to continue in their studies help matters? This flies in the face of evidence of how children react to a compulsory curriculum (Kelly, 1990 pp. 90-109). Moreover, these disaffected children are likely to undermine the work of those who do wish to study these subjects—either by distracting them in mixed-ability classes, or by undermining the morale of their teachers: it is not easy forcing 15-year olds to keep on with subjects in studying which ten previous years of schooling have failed to instil any pleasure.

What might raise standards would be improved teaching methods to help children overcome their difficulties. Work has been done in these areas in both maths and science (see for example, in maths, Mason and Tooley, 1992). Could it not be argued, then, that what is needed is a national curriculum which ensured that the best of such teaching methods were disseminated? However, neither the current National Curriculum, nor the proposals of the IPPR, want to impinge upon teachers' choice of teaching method. Rightly, I think, they balk at undermining teachers' autonomy in this crucial area. But why should not teachers' autonomy be overridden if this would ensure the raising of standards? There are two immediate problems with this. First, there just is not the agreed pedagogy with which to raise standards. The methods used are controversial. This brings us to the problem of the knowledge of the curriculum planners—an issue which will be taken up below. Secondly, even in the unlikely event of the experts agreeing, to impose new methods on teachers is likely to backfire: 'attempts at innovation do not work if the teacher is seen, and is treated, as a largely passive recipient of change and innovation planned on his or her behalf by others' (Kelly, 1990 p. 105). So what would be needed, if areas are perceived to be nationally weak, is for national initiatives to find better ways of teaching, and to disseminate these methods, through initial teacher and in-service training. If teachers are convinced that these methods work, then they will use them as intended. If they are not, they will not, and no amount of legislation will ensure that they do. A national curriculum, even one which specified teaching methods, will not raise standards in this way.

## Raising standards 2: setting clear objectives

The second claim of the Government is that their National Curriculum will raise standards by 'setting clear objectives for what children over the full range of ability should be able to achieve ... This will help schools to challenge each child to develop his or her potential ... pupils can be stretched further when they are doing well and given more help when they are not' (DES, 1987 pp. 3-4). Again, the IPPR's emphasis on coherence and clarity in its objectives might be expected to raise standards in the same way.

Now, the 'clear objectives' set in the National Curriculum point to levels of attainment which an average child should be achieving for his or her age, and the likely range in which children of that age will fall. The 'guesses' of these levels in the current National Curriculum should not be taken too seriously; they were not based on much research evidence. However, the principle, if not the particulars, of stipulated levels is likely to be the same for any national curriculum. So how will they help to challenge children? A teacher of an 11-year old boy, say, at level 2, realises that an average child of his age should be at level 4. So should the teacher challenge him to do better? Again, the issue of professional autonomy arises. For the teacher might know that the child in question is already working at maximum capacity, and that what is needed is not comparisons with children of average ability, but praise for doing so well. Similarly a girl who is at level 4 may require the teacher to praise her a great deal, but equally she may need to be cajoled into doing better, depending on whether she is of average, or above-average, ability. Without levels given by a national curriculum, good teachers will already have reasonable ideas about these matters, based on the traditions of teaching within which they have been initiated.

To suppose that simply publishing average levels of attainment will lead 'poorer' teachers to stretch their children seems rather far-fetched. A teacher who underestimates the potential of, say, Afro-Caribbean children, is not suddenly going to react to them differently because there are now published levels for the average child: the teacher has reacted to them with low expectations *precisely because he or she has assumed that the children are below average!* With or without published levels, the teacher can carry on doing this. But could it not be argued that parents can now see that the teachers are doing their children a disservice? This is an important point, and ties in with my later argument about the checks and balances needed on the professionalism of teachers. But, although reflecting on national levels of attainment might be useful here, there seem far easier—but less codifiable—ways of ascertaining that ones' children are not being stretched. For example, sensitivity towards ones' children's reactions to schooling—are they bored or challenged? Or simple comparisons with other children in the school, perhaps of a different race, could provide similar information.

Again, setting clear national objectives does not seem to be a useful way of raising standards. The final way that a national curriculum might raise standards is by giving equal opportunities to all—this issue is now addressed.

## Equality of opportunity

The Conservative Government stressed: 'Pupils should be entitled to the same opportunities wherever they go to school' (DES and WO, 1987 p. 3). These sentiments pervade the IPPR's treatment of their national curriculum, as the title of *A National Curriculum for all* suggests. Moreover, this equal entitlement was suggested by the Conservative Government as being one way in which standards can be raised: by 'ensuring that all pupils, regardless of sex, ethnic origin and geographical location, have access to broadly the same good and relevant curriculum' (ibid.).

Equality of opportunity seems to be an extremely powerful argument for a national curriculum. If some schools are failing to provide some pupils with access to a 'good' curriculum, or some children within schools are not given such access, then this is highly unfair. Also it seems plausible that standards could be raised by ensuring that access to a good education is granted to all. But the important question seems to be: is a national curriculum the best way of raising the level of those 'failing' schools? Let us consider different types of 'failing' school, and see if a national curriculum could help.

The first could be of the 'William Tyndale'-type. That is, a school which many parents and children feel to be offering an inappropriate curriculum—in this case, not enough concentration on the basics of literacy and numeracy, and too much devotion to such issues as anti-racism and egalitarianism. Now presumably a national curriculum which was *highly prescriptive and effectively policed,* could effectively rule out that sort of curriculum. A less prescriptive or less well policed national curriculum might not do so, for again, empirical evidence suggests that teachers are likely to 'cannibalise' and 'sabotage' imposed curricula which are not to their liking (Kelly, 1990 p. 105). With the current National Curriculum, for example, it would be easy to teach mathematics totally through 'anti-racist'-maths examples. Or a completely loose 'discovery' teaching method could be employed, for nowhere are teaching methods stipulated. Now, it is important to stress that schools like 'William Tyndale' are the exception not the rule (Ball, 1990 p. 26). Why bludgeon all schools into submitting to a highly prescriptive and heavily policed national curriculum when it is only a few schools which are 'erring' in this way? Would specific action not be more preferable? Indeed, this was how the 'problem' of William Tyndale was tackled, with HMI and local authority inspections, followed by guidance on changes that were required.

Would the inspectorate not need to consult some national curriculum documentation and point to how the school is failing in terms of this provision, in order to put things right? No, the inspectorate do not work in an educational vacuum. They are already imbued with a culture and tradition which gives them curriculum criteria from which to work. They do not need outsiders prescribing to them the details of a curriculum of which they already have both tacit and explicit knowledge.

A final query might be of how such 'problem' schools get identified, if there is not a national curriculum to point to. Again, this supposes parents and children existing in an educational vacuum. There is widespread acceptance that, for example, a principal purpose of primary schools is to teach literacy and numeracy. Parents will soon cotton on to the fact that the performance of their schools is not up to scratch. Once defects are spotted, there are two ways in which attention can be brought to schools which seem to be failing. The first is through the 'voice' option—complaining to the headteacher, the governors, the local authority, or MP, or the media. This was how the William Tyndale episode was brought to light. Or parents can now exercise the right of 'exit'—by moving to another school; with the child goes its *per capita* funding. If enough pupils leave in this way, signals are sent to the local authority or DFE that something is amiss. Perhaps more significantly, market signals are sent to the school management itself, in terms of reduced revenue, to let them know that they are not delivering the curriculum that parents and children require. These issues will be taken up in the last section. But it does not seem that a national curriculum would help these kinds of schools very much.

A second sort of 'failing' school problem a national curriculum might be thought to address would be 'sink' schools—schools that deteriorate so much that they provide a totally inadequate education for their pupils. I suggest that the problems in such schools are caused by poor management, or by lack of resources, or both. The unsatisfactory curriculum will be a symptom of this, not the cause. Of course, an imposed curriculum might help such schools—but exactly the same considerations as above would question whether it therefore follows that all schools have to have a curriculum similarly imposed.

But what about this crucial issue of more resources? It is popular for the political right to condemn the left for assuming that all problems can be solved 'by throwing more money at the problem'. What they mean is that extra resources in themselves are not enough, they must be managed and targeted carefully. Now, crucially, a national curriculum takes funds from the education budget, and distributes these resources willy-nilly between schools. The school with the excellent academic reputation has the same resources devoted to it through the national curriculum, as the underachieving school in the inner city. Why is this the best solution to the problem of the 'failing' school? Would it not be far better to target resources where they are most needed?

The resources in question are not trivial: the current National Curriculum costs ten million pounds per year from central government funds—4 per cent of the total schools' budget. If we add in funds spent on national testing, then we get 14 per cent of the total central government budget allocated to schools (DES, 1991; SEAC, 1991; NCC, 1990). If there are 100 'sink' schools, ten million pounds could provide *five extra teachers to each 'sink' school*. Would that not be a better way of targeting schools in need than to distribute the funds to all schools, most of which have perfectly satisfactory curricula already? In fact, the current National Curriculum costs much more than that—Coopers and Lybrand Deloitte estimated that primary schools spent an extra £671 million per year, plus a start-up cost of £1,300 million (*Times Educational Supplement*, 6 December 1991 and 17 January 1992).

Now perhaps it might be argued that it is just this particular national curriculum that is so expensive, but that others would be cheaper? The IPPR says that their curriculum will be less prescriptive, and hence presumably cheaper (O'Hear and White, 1991 p. 10). I doubt this. For a start, it was not the Conservative government's intention to have such a prescriptive curriculum either—Mrs.

Thatcher herself bemoaned the excessive detail that emerged from her committees (*Sunday Telegraph*, 1 April 1990, quoted Aldrich (1992) p. 60). What is likely is that committees in a democracy will produce excessive prescription, because of the problems of political uncertainty. Those who win political power have it guaranteed only for a short time, creating an incentive to insulate policies from future democratic control. Once a curriculum, for example, becomes law, it is 'part of the *status quo* that the system inherently works to protect' (Chubb and Moe, 1990 p. 42). It would be politically inexpedient for a new government to inconvenience schools by imposing a different national curriculum on them. What they can do, though, is change the details. This creates incentives to avoid discretionary aspects of laws: 'The best way for groups to protect their achievements from the uncertainties of future politics, therefore, is through formalization: the formal reduction or elimination of discretion, and the formal insulation of any remaining discretion from future political influence' (ibid., pp. 42-3). This pressure leads to committees going for exactly the detailed prescription that the IPPR says it will avoid.

One other pressure within democratic control is also relevant here—the need for compromise. The committees set up by a government to formulate the national curriculum are likely to consist of people from varying political backgrounds. So, some compromises will be needed. But compromises are 'agreements among contending, often mutually suspicious, sides that can easily come apart over time if they are informal and subject to discretion' (ibid., p. 44). Opposing groups wanting to insure against these dangers put 'everything in writing, down to the last detail, and make it legally enforceable—to formalize the agreement' (ibid.). Chubb and Moe give an example of a nine-page federal government statute for aid to disadvantaged students generating 174 pages of statutory amendments. This explosion of detailed prescription is, I suggest, what would happen to the IPPR's lean national curriculum, exactly as happened with the current National Curriculum. With this level of prescription will come the expense, and with it the diversion of resources away from where they are truly needed.

A national curriculum will not bring equality of opportunity. It is likely to divert resources from where they are needed, diffusing them around the school population at large. The IPPR's espousal of this policy seems rather odd for that reason alone.

## Coherence and continuity

Without a national curriculum the IPPR argue that there are 'too few mechanisms for matching what [is] learnt between primary and secondary schools, or even between one class and the next' (O'Hear and White, 1991 p. 5). Similarly, the Government argued that their National Curriculum would ensure 'that the curriculum offered in all maintained schools has sufficient in common to enable children to move from one area of the country to another with minimum disruption to their education. It will also help children's progression within and between primary and secondary education ... and will help to secure the continuity and coherence which is too often lacking in what they are taught' (DES and WO, 1987 p. 4).

Now a *very prescriptive* national curriculum, dictating what topics were to be taught in each week, say, could solve these problems. But as far as the less prescriptive National Curriculum or the IPPR's alternative are concerned, it is hard to see how they will make any difference to this problem. Because of the latitude given to schools, the geographically mobile are still 'liable to encounter "Dinosaurs" or "The Vikings" three or four times during their primary schooling' (Kirk, 1986 p. 38).

Moreover, even as regards continuity between primary and secondary schools, or between years in each school, it is hard to see how anything but a very prescriptive national curriculum will help. The current National Curriculum does not prescribe in which year topics must be covered. It will still be possible for children to be taught at secondary school what they have already covered before in primary school. It might be argued that the National Curriculum will facilitate records of work covered, in language that all schools can understand in terms of levels and attainment targets. Hence these will encourage schools to base their teaching accordingly. But this assumption is naïve in several ways. First, that teachers will take much notice of these records and plan teaching accordingly: good teachers will, but it is likely they will have made some effort anyway to plan teaching in this way, through liaison with feeder schools and diagnostic assessment of children. Poorer teachers probably will not, irrespective of whether there is this legislation.

Second, it embodies questionable notions about children's learning: some children can absorb something on first encountering it, while others need more exposure.

Many children can go through a course, even pass tests in it, without really understanding it. Particularly in hierarchical subjects such as mathematics, it is not enough to know that someone has covered an earlier topic, what is needed is to know that the child *understands* the relevant concepts *now*. So what is really needed for curriculum coherence is for teachers to use a *diagnostic teaching method*, discovering their pupils' understanding in relevant areas before moving to something new. As we have seen, it is unlikely that dissemination of such teaching methods could simply be accomplished by legislating for them in a national curriculum. Moreover, neither the current National Curriculum, nor that envisaged by the IPPR, prescribe teaching methods. As they stand, then, neither seems to be a particularly effective mechanism for ensuring curriculum continuity and coherence.

## Economic competitiveness

Concern about international economic competitiveness was an important factor leading to the introduction of the National Curriculum. The IPPR also argue that this is one motivation for their national curriculum: 'we cannot survive as a major industrial nation without far higher levels of relevant knowledge and skill in the workforce'. Moreover, 'it is reasonable to claim that the hit-and-miss curricula of the old laissez-faire system' were less likely to facilitate economic competitiveness 'than a properly thought-through and coordinated national framework' (O'Hear and White, 1991 p. 5).

One of the concerns is clearly that of skills in mathematics, science and technology—the unlikelihood of a national curriculum raising standards in these areas has already been discussed. What is needed to raise the levels of knowledge in these areas would be better teaching methods, not a broad and balanced national curriculum.

One common response is, since many of our international competitors have compulsory core curricula, that is what we need too. This assumes a very simplistic causal connection between a nation's curriculum and its industrial output. But in both Japan and France—two of our competitors—there is concern that the *rigidity* and *inflexibility* of their national curricula might be detrimental to industrial innovation and lead to underachievement (Kelly, 1990 p. 125 and *Times Educational Supplement* 6 December 1992, p. 22). These nations might be economically competitive in spite of, not because of, their national curricula. This brings us to the central problem of the knowledge of the curriculum planners. We live, as we are frequently told, in a fast-changing world. A curriculum imposed now is likely, because of political exigencies, to be in place well into the next century. How can the central curriculum planners satisfactorily take into account economic and technological uncertainties, and predict what a relevant curriculum will be then?

I have surveyed each of the arguments concerned with the problems of state education. None point to a national curriculum as a solution. Indeed, particularly in the cases of raising standards, promoting equality of opportunity, and economic competitiveness, it seems more plausible that a national curriculum would have a detrimental impact. We now move on to consider the 'positive' philosophical reasons given in support, to see if they fare any better.

## THE CASE FOR A NATIONAL CURRICULUM: PHILOSOPHICAL ARGUMENTS

The first philosophical argument, concerned with the nature of *knowledge*, can be quickly dismissed. Knowledge, it is claimed, is differentiated into various 'forms', and to be educated, a person must be initiated into each of these forms. Hence, 'schools should make provision for pupils to be systematically initiated into all of them' (Kirk, 1986 p. 33). Professor Hirst has now repudiated his classic outline of this position (Hirst, 1992), which demonstrates well the problem the curriculum planners would have in reaching consensus devising a curriculum along these lines. But there is a bigger problem with this as a justification for a state-imposed curriculum. Just because knowledge might be constructed in a particular way tells us nothing about whether or not the state should intervene to impose initiation into that knowledge. What is needed is some political or moral justification for that. We have already looked at the argument for equality of opportunity, which we considered as a *negative* objection to life without a national curriculum, but which could equally have found its way into this section. The argument about the nature of knowledge would need to be supplemented with the injunction that equality of opportunity would be violated if some children were not initiated into all the forms of knowledge. But then the arguments already encountered would apply against this position.

The other philosophical arguments for a compulsory core curriculum concern democratic control of the curriculum, education for participation in democracy, and education for autonomy. Each of these will now be considered.

## Democratic control of the curriculum

This is the major preoccupation of the IPPR's curriculum proposals. Without democratic control, one group of people, professional educationalists, will have control of an area which is of crucial importance to all. The argument has a long vintage in White's earlier writings. The IPPR's formulation begins:

> 'The main argument for shifting from professional to political control of the broad framework of the curriculum is that questions about the aims and content of the curriculum are intimately connected with views about the kind of society we wish to live in. They are as much political questions as issues of taxation policy or defence.' (O'Hear and White, 1991 p. 10).

In an earlier work (1981 p. 257), White clarified that there is no *necessary* connection between something having political implications and the need for political control. He agreed with the observation that 'a political theory may incorporate in itself the view that the agenda of matters deserving of government control should be limited' (Dearden, 1980 p. 153). So just because the curriculum is 'intimately connected' with the notion of the good society, it does not *necessarily* follow that decisions about the curriculum must be made by the body politic. What is needed is 'a review of the various contingent factors at a particular historical time' (White, 1981 p. 257), to ascertain whether or not political control is a good idea. Now what seems to have emerged in White's writings is that the contingent factor is *democracy*: in a democracy, issues of political equality are paramount. The argument of the IPPR thus continues:

> 'Every citizen in a democracy should have an equal right to participate in the control or exercise of political power in these and other areas ... the citizenry as a whole, not the teachers, should decide the overall shape of school curricula.' (O'Hear and White, 1991 p. 10).

Does this emphasis on democracy give a strong reason for political control of the curriculum? Much depends on the 'contingent factors' of the particular democracy.

Now, in our democracy, political control is exercised through the ballot box, and lobbying of Parliament. When an election is called, political parties liaise with their professional educationalists, and produce educational policies for the manifestos. The ordinary voter will have played no part in formulating these. At most there will be a few lines about the curriculum, together with a few lines about all of the other educational issues, and a few lines about every other issue of concern to the government. In the 1992 Labour Party manifesto, education in total covered two pages. Of this, *one paragraph* concerned the curriculum, a paragraph notable only for its blandness. Hardly enough to enable all citizens to engage in the debate. Moreover, individual voters have only one vote to express their opinions about a range of issues. It is unlikely that the curriculum influences the vote of many.

If we follow the passage of legislation through the political process, we find that there is not such a sharp contrast to be made between 'professional' and 'political' control, the dichotomy suggested by White. For professional educationalists impinge upon the process at all levels: they influence the formulation of legislation—via the Department for Education (DFE), and lobbying of Parliament—they are entrusted with 'fleshing out' proposals and carrying policies into schools. This seems a far cry from all voters having an equal right to influence the process, a far cry from control of the curriculum 'by all sections of the citizenry'.

Presumably, the IPPR has in mind a more active, participatory democracy. But given the 'contingent factors' of our actual democracy, the need for democratic control of the curriculum fades in importance. Indeed, the need for government control of the curriculum at all is called into question, as White elsewhere agrees:

> 'It does not follow ... that the wisest policy in any liberal democracy is to put the aims of education under government control. For actual governments may not be motivated by the desire to help everyone to become autonomous ... Whether or not aims should be left to government cannot be laid down by a formula. Everything depends on local considerations ... Where a government is likely to misuse its power, to mouth autonomy for all, for instance, but in reality to encourage autonomy for a few and structure the educational system so that the many become their servants, then the move would be unwise.' (White, 1988 p. 230).

My suggestion, then, is that in our society, the difference between 'political' control and 'professional' control is very slight in terms of the formulation of the policy, and hence hardly an important justification for state control of the curriculum. In both cases the same sorts of institutions are at work creating and modifying the outcome. Under 'political' control the role of the individual voter is simply to choose the party which chooses the executive which liaises with the 'professional' bodies to decide the curriculum. The voter also gets to ratify or reject this decision, amongst a myriad other decisions, by voting for or against the government at the next election. But though this difference is slight, there is a more significant difference of course. For under 'political' control, the outcome becomes law, to be policed and administered, and with possibly unforeseen negative repercussions. These issues will be dealt with below. In a better, more ideal, democracy, there might be more of a case for democratic control. I suggest that until we arrive in that state, we can hardly adopt this as a justification for a national curriculum.

## Effective participation in democracy

The second philosophical argument considers the needs of citizens for effective participation in democracy. This is related to, but not identical with, the argument addressed below, of the importance of 'autonomy for all' in a liberal democracy.

One formulation is set out by Crick and Porter: 'we have to teach or let the pupils learn skills relevant to political action ... it is common sense and common prudence to develop political literacy as a general educational and cultural goal' (Crick and Porter, 1978 pp. 6-7). They go on to argue that a 'politically literate person would possess, among other things, a knowledge of those concepts minimally necessary to construct simple conceptual and analytical frameworks' (ibid. p. 47), and spell this out as requiring, *inter alia*, the development of oral and written language skills, an understanding of number and statistics, the scientific interpretation of data, and ethical understanding (ibid. p. 255).

The argument is that democracy needs its citizens to be educated in this knowledge and these skills in order to function properly. Hence, the democratic state must ensure that all its citizens are so educated, through a national curriculum. I offer three arguments against this position—the last of which I will mention in passing.

First, it is likely that the list of requirements for participation will be both controversial and hence very detailed. Controversy will clearly arise because the notion of a participatory democracy—however weakly defined—is only one interpretation of democracy, and the battlelines over this and other interpretations are already drawn. Opposing philosophies would dispute the notion of skills, knowledge and qualities that are needed for participation (see, for example, Riker, 1982, and Tooley, 1991). The considerations discussed above, under equality of opportunity, suggested that matters of great controversy will need more detailed prescription, for reasons of both political preservation and achieving of compromise. More detailed prescriptive curricula will undermine teachers' autonomy and professionalism, and are likely to be more open to sabotage and a low level of implementation. For these reasons, this argument for a national curriculum should be viewed cautiously.

Second, the list of requirements for participation in a democracy is likely to be very long indeed—as the work of Crick and Porter suggests. Consequently, the national curriculum is likely to be very extensive, and the majority of citizens are unlikely to become acquainted with more than a small subset of it. (Consider the political decision, even in our restricted democracy, on how to vote at a general election. Think of the issues in economics, international relations, education, the environment, ethics, and so on, that would need to be considered. Think of how little qualified most of us are to do this.)

Some might object that a *grounding* in these issues for all would be better than nothing, and improve the quality of our democracy. I doubt this. I frequently find that my views on a subject change, the more in-depth knowledge I acquire. Take a topical theme such as the environment. Perhaps the minimum level of education for participation in democracy would inform children about the hole in the ozone layer and how government action on pollution could solve this problem; those with this minimum level of education might then vote for the party which supported, say, strong European pollution controls on industry. Someone with a little more information might discover that the hole is over Antarctica, and hence question how the industrial pollution of the 'North' could have caused it. They might then discover that some experts suggest instead it is caused by volcanic activity in the 'South'. Or a more advanced education might lead one to see disagreeable effects of combined government action in Europe to reduce pollution, and hence to question whether or not there might be other, and better, ways of combating it. (Current European legislation leads to the perverse effect of outlawing the lean-burn engine, which is considerably cleaner than an engine fitted with a catalytic convertor. Indeed, catalytic convertors make things *worse* at average European morning temperatures, although they are quite effective at average temperatures in California, where they were tested.) My point is that a little information is not necessarily any better than none. *Understanding* of issues is what is required for informed political decision making, not a passing acquaintance with a few bare facts.

The third issue might seem a little esoteric, so I mention it in passing. If the stipulated skills, knowledge and personal qualities are *necessary* for participation in democracy, what should be done with those who fail to obtain them? Should they be allowed to vote or otherwise participate in democracy? I have argued elsewhere that the logic of the position is that they should not (Tooley, 1990). The basic argument is that if these qualities are important enough for governments to override autonomy in curricular matters, then governments are neglecting their duty to educated citizens if those who have failed to obtain their 'education adequate for participation in democracy' are allowed to participate.

The usual argument against this position is that this would be undemocratic, and hence, although it might be *desirable* that all citizens had an 'education adequate for participation in democracy', we must stop at enforcing this as a condition for voting and other participation. I argue that this does not hold, but I will not go into this now. But even if the details of that argument were not accepted, still it must be noted that the case for a compulsory core curriculum has been considerably undermined: for we seem to have the position that, although the ideal might be that *all* citizens have the education adequate for participation, in practice it must be a matter of degree. (This is so, because those without the required education are still allowed to participate.) But then without a national curriculum, there will also be a (large?) proportion of citizens with the relevant skills, knowledge, and personal qualities for participation. The argument could boil down to haggling over whether more people will have these with, or without, a national curriculum.

Whether or not this third argument is found convincing, the first two considerations suggest that using 'education adequate for participation in a democracy' as a justification for a compulsory core curriculum is flawed. Taking it seriously would result in a far too detailed, prescriptive and extensive curriculum.

This would alienate both students and teachers: the former because few would be able to master it, the latter because of its effect of undermining their autonomy.

## Autonomy for all

A related, but not identical motivation for a national curriculum concerns the needs of all citizens in a liberal democracy for autonomy. It is not that autonomy is simply required for participation in a democracy, but that it is required to live a 'good life' at all. This is the argument of the IPPR and of John White.

White argues that the state has a role in three areas, the third of which is germane for our purposes: 'in order to become autonomous one needs to have acquired various capacities, dispositions, and types of understanding. If a government is committed to the promotion of autonomy for everyone, its aim must be that everyone should be educated to enable them to exercise it.' (White, 1990 p. 23). This is the justification for government intervention in a national curriculum.

Why should a government be committed to promoting autonomy in the first place? We shall skip over this issue here, or whether it is likely that any democratic government would be concerned with it. We give White and the IPPR the benefit of the doubt and see what follows.

I find problems with these proposals in two main areas. First, I suggest that a state-controlled curriculum for autonomy will have a detrimental impact on the autonomy of schools and teachers, and hence, of students. Second, that other autonomy-promoting institutions of civil society will be undermined by a national curriculum for autonomy.

The first of these reservations is perhaps not as obvious as it appears. Indeed, as we have noted, O'Hear and White are at pains to stress that their curriculum proposals, *unlike* the current National Curriculum, *will* leave substantial control of the curriculum to schools and teachers: 'The new curriculum we are proposing will give considerable powers back to the schools within defensible national constraints' (O'Hear and White, 1991 p. 11). This is of considerable importance to them, because children learn by example, and if they see their teachers heavily constrained by the state, this will influence the lessons they imbibe about autonomy and democratic participation: White notes 'we know that children learn by example and are more likely to acquire a taste for the autonomous life from people who themselves embody it than from the hemmed-in functionaries within an authoritarian system' (White, 1990 p. 132). However, I have suggested above that whenever there is controversy and the need for compromise, the exigencies of democracy mean that heavily prescribed legislation will be the outcome. And it is clear that there is highly likely to be controversy about what makes up an 'education for autonomy'. For White and O'Hear, the crucial element of their 'curriculum for autonomy' lies in the development of personal qualities. From these, knowledge and understanding, experience of the arts and practical competencies are derived. But have they adequately located all those, and only those, qualities necessary for autonomy? For example, we might wonder whether their 'temperance' was a necessary condition for an autonomous person, or whether without a 'contemplative reflectiveness ... on our existential characteristics as self-conscious creatures aware of our mortality' (O'Hear and White, 1991 p. 13), we should forgo the label of autonomous.

The crucial point in the context here is that with any curriculum for autonomy there is likely to be controversy, and with it the likelihood of a *highly prescribed curriculum*. Hence, the proposed 'education for autonomy' will have the paradoxical effect, because of its controversial nature, of firmly curtailing the autonomy of teachers and schools, even though this was not a desired outcome. With the curtailment of this autonomy comes the undermining of the autonomy of pupils, for the reasons given by White.

My second argument is that, by prescribing a compulsory 'curriculum for autonomy', other autonomy-reinforcing agencies in society will be undermined. First, I suggest that it would be agreed by O'Hear and White that although citizens do not necessarily acquire *all* of the desired qualities of the autonomous person, they do acquire *some* of them. For example, the great majority of children I suspect will develop the 'qualities of character', such as courage, self-control, patience, etc. Similarly, children generally will enjoy physical pleasures, the company of others, working with others, and so on. As we go down the IPPR's list we will find pockets of inadequacy, not wholesale swathes of need. The IPPR has offered us no empirical evidence, or even a thought experiment, to try and ascertain which of its desired qualities will be commonly present, which ones absent. Importantly, it *does not see the need to do so*. It is outlining the desirable qualities for the autonomous person. The curriculum must ensure that all are inculcated in these values, now and in the future. Hence, whether or not many, even most, children are obtaining these qualities without government intervention, the compulsory curriculum should still be instituted.

This position would be unobjectionable if it was assumed that government intervention is costless. That is, not only in terms of monetary costs, but also in terms of side-effects, including that of the extension of government power itself. Here, I cannot make this assumption. Vast amounts of literature point to the possible negative and unforeseen effects of government intervention, from theoretical and empirical perspectives (see, for a taste, West, 1970, on intervention in education; Green, 1985, on medical issues; Murray, 1984, on welfare provision; Sowell, 1990, on 'positive discrimination'; and Matthews and Benjamin, 1992, on economic policy). Hence, any extension of government powers will be viewed cautiously here. The guiding principle will be that if something can be obtained *without* government intervention, then this is preferable to obtaining it *through* intervention. So, unlike for the IPPR, for me it is an important question whether, and to what extent, the qualities of the autonomous citizen are being met, before a great extension of government powers is sought.

Now, where might people acquire their 'education for autonomy'? I suggest through the institutions of 'civil society': families, communities, religious groups, markets, the media, friends, and lone activities. White seems to agree: he argues that 'the content of education embraces more than the timetabled curriculum. At its broadest, it includes what children learn from their parents and the media' (White, 1990 p. 142). He accepts that much of the 'education for autonomy' *could* and *is likely* to be learnt out of school. Now in the rarefied atmosphere of the academic book, he goes on to suggest that, therefore, 'I ... argue that there needs to be state regulation not only of timetabled activities, but also of educational vehicles such as these [the media and the family]'. However, perhaps aware of the startling political implications of this, these suggestions are largely dropped from the IPPR pamphlet. But this means that a great deal is being crammed into the *school* curriculum that should not really be there. For example, it is noted that the personal qualities could be arrived at in the 'home, at school and in the community' (O'Hear and White, 1991 p. 11). But the emphasis throughout the IPPR document is on getting these qualities at school.

So we are left with the conclusion that a national curriculum which extensively regulated the family, church, friendships, etc., as well as the school, may well be a suitable vehicle for ensuring that all children were exposed to the qualities needed for autonomy. Let us call this 'totalitarianism', and await a defence of it from institutions such as the IPPR. But notice that, without it, something rather peculiar happens. A national curriculum for autonomy is restricted to schools. Two ramifications follow from this. First, schools are unlikely to be a good place to obtain an 'education for autonomy'—there might be very sound psychological and practical reasons why the school is not the best place for the development of these qualities. For example, classrooms might be too large, or teachers not the right people to talk over issues with. Or, as research has shown (Kelly, 1990), compulsory curriculum subjects will not necessarily be absorbed by students, and their presence may actually serve to alienate them. But second, and most significantly, not only might children be receiving an inferior 'education for autonomy' than that obtained in other institutions, but crucially, these other institutions might themselves become undermined. For example, if many of the personal qualities listed are assumed to be the school's responsibility, children might consult or confide in their parents less. Or parents might feel that it is not their role to instil these qualities in their children, because it is by law the school's role. Or the educational experts might warn parents that their 'common sense' parenting methods were not good enough, and so it was best to leave such education to school. The last two comments are not at all far-fetched—they have both happened in the case of reading and sex education. In other words, I am suggesting that a national curriculum in schools geared to autonomy might actually serve to undermine it, by undermining other institutions that already serve autonomy, or that could be strengthened to serve autonomy.

Hence, my conclusions in this section are that there might be very real difficulties with using a compulsory national curriculum to promote autonomy. Some of the desirable qualities listed by the IPPR may not be found in some children, but this does not mean that we can simply place them on the school curriculum, and assume that the problem is solved. One way of promoting autonomy without a national curriculum will be discussed in the concluding section.

*James Tooley*

## KNOWLEDGE AND DECISIONS

The discussion so far has looked at the major reasons given for a compulsory national curriculum, both negative and positive, and has found each justification to be inadequate. One issue which has cropped up several times is that of the knowledge of the curriculum planners. This, and the related concern about levels of decision making, will now be discussed. They are issues which serve further to undermine the case for a national curriculum.

### The knowledge of the curriculum planners

Suppose the Labour Party had won the election in 1992, and the IPPR's national curriculum had been viewed favourably by the new administration. How would the central curriculum planners have proceeded? They would have had

> 'to work out a coherent and defensible set of overall aims; examine what sub-aims, or intermediate aims, these might generate on logical, psychological and other grounds; bear in mind the wide variety of ways by which aims might be realized; and try to work out criteria delimiting the role of central government from that of local government, governing bodies and schools... all of which would be *a long and massive undertaking*, requiring the collaboration of professionals, civil servants, politicians and others in some kind of semi-independent but politically accountable national educational council' (White, 1990 p. 13, my italics).

My question is: would it have been too long and massive an undertaking? Let us follow the planning process through, and see the sorts of problems that might arise.

### *The make-up of the committees*

First problem: who would be on the many committees and sub-committees? For the choice of those people could largely determine the result of the deliberations. Will they be people who largely agree on political issues, or will there be a balance of political colour, and hence great difficulties in reaching agreement? Kenneth Baker, the architect of the 1988 Act, oddly appointed a committee of left-leaning people, with whom he could not agree. This was then 'rectified' by one of his successors, Kenneth Clarke. If compromises need to be made, then this is likely to lead to excessively detailed legislation, far from what the IPPR seeks.

## *'Tacit' knowledge*

Next problem: can the knowledge needed by the central planners be articulated? For there is a long tradition in political philosophy which queries whether much knowledge about society is of this articulated form, or whether it is knowledge that is 'tacit', discovered only through practices and traditions (see for example: Hayek, 1960; Oakeshott, 1962; Polanyi, 1958). A brief look at a couple of the IPPR's criteria which 'any adequate national curriculum must satisfy' (O'Hear and White, 1991 p. 5) will illustrate the sorts of problems I have in mind.

The IPPR says that a national curriculum 'must have a clear and defensible set of general aims, linked to the personal, civic and economic expectations of the national community'. What does it mean for a 'national community' to have expectations of its citizens?[1] How can we discover what these expectations are? Can they be articulated for use in the committee room as envisaged by the IPPR? A national curriculum 'must be directed towards promoting success rather than identifying and reinforcing failure'. Is the ability to do this not a practice which depends on the feel of the teacher in the classroom, rather than the articulations of central planners? And so on. Each of their criteria seems to present problems over articulation of what takes place in the teacher-pupil relationship, or with pupils in schools.

It is interesting to note in this context how White seems off the mark when he argues that the 1988 National Curriculum was devised much too quickly, with far too little thought given to the aims and content of the curriculum. The Government 'showed that devising a national curriculum is simplicity itself. You pick ten foundation subjects to fill most of the school timetable, highlight three as of particular importance and arrange for tests at different ages. I could have worked out the national curriculum years ago. Anyone could.' (White, 1990 p. 13). The assumption here is that not enough articulated, rational planning in committee rooms took place, hence there was not enough planning at all. On the contrary, I suggest that the process of devising the current National Curriculum took place over many centuries, up to about 1904. Aldrich (1992 p. 67) has noted how the 1988 National Curriculum is virtually a copy of the curriculum directives of 1904.

But prior to that, without any state intervention in the curriculum (except for the abortive attempt at 'payment by results' in the 1860s), a curriculum had *evolved* through centuries of 'social experimentation' (Watson, 1909). Through a process of 'natural selection' and 'adaptation', the curriculum evolved out of the education of the gentleman, tempered with the ethos of discipline from the grammar schools and an orientation to the world of work. The committees of 1904 simply formalised this unarticulated 'knowledge' contained within the traditions of society. But of course, they did not—and could not—formalise everything. Much was taken for granted about the way schools were at the time, including the details of ethos and organisation. The 1988 committees simply latched onto those traditions. Of course, it is questionable whether they were relevant 84 years later. However, the point is that knowledge does not have to be articulated to be useful and used.

## The 'Renaissance Person' problem

Even if the knowledge, or some part of it, can be articulated *within separate disciplines*, will the experts from these different fields be able to communicate with each other, and understand each other? For the great expansion of knowledge means that there can no longer be a 'Renaissance Person', familiar with all fields. 'The more civilised we become,' says Hayek, 'the more relatively ignorant must each individual be of the facts on which the working of his civilisation depends. The very division of knowledge increases the necessary ignorance of the individual of most of this knowledge' (Hayek, 1960 p. 26). This has profound implications for any central curriculum planners, who will be largely ignorant of all but one of the disciplines brought to bear on the planning, such as economics, history, curriculum subjects, philosophy, psychology, politics, and so on (in fact, their specialised knowledge will, of course, be limited to a small subset of one of these disciplines). How will these people on committees communicate with each other, and weigh up their different claims?

## Reaching decisions

How will the committees reach their decisions? Is it assumed that they will achieve consensus? Presumably not, so will majority voting carry the day on something so important? What voting system will they use? How do they know that this does not have malfunctions, which will render the outcome of their deliberations void of any meaning? I have written about the problems of voting elsewhere (Tooley, 1991). The general result is that all voting systems have the possibility of severe malfunctions. This may lead to the committee members all preferring some option which does not get chosen, or of the eventual choice being an arbitrary one.

### Getting it right

Now, remembering that the outcome of the national curriculum committees' work is legislation to be implemented in all schools, affecting all of the nation's children, and hence the nation itself for the next few generations: what confidence can we have that the planners will get it right? Suppose the committee is made up of very wise members, say with a 0.9 probability of getting any one particular decision correct. Suppose they have to make decisions about 10 major and statistically independent issues. Then, the probability of being right on the whole package is $(\frac{9}{10})^{10}$, just 0.3487. That is, this very wise committee deciding on ten important issues has only a probability of about one third of getting everything right. That is, it is very likely to get at least one of the important decisions wrong. A wrong decision will then be made law and forced to be implemented in all schools. This probability, of course, sharply increases when we consider less wise committees. For example, if on each issue, the probability of getting things right is 0.75, then on ten issues, the probability of getting everything right is $(\frac{3}{4})^{10}$ or 0.056, which is a very tiny probability indeed.

### Unintended consequences

Even if it is assumed that the central planners can put forward a plausible articulation, and even if this could be comprehensible across different disciplines, can we be sure that it will not have unintended consequences that may undermine the policy? One minor example of this has already been noted—the desire for a broad and balanced primary curriculum may have led to a decline in reading standards. Again, as previously noted, the IPPR's emphasis on a curriculum that promotes autonomy could well lead to the undermining of other institutions that currently serve autonomy.

The general point is that given the complexity of our social system, we just cannot be sure how different aspects interrelate, and how changes in one area will affect other areas and institutions. It might be thought that if there are effective, fast and accurate feedback mechanisms, then counterproductive policies can be quickly discovered, and altered. But this, then, brings in the appropriate levels of decision-making about education. For crucially, the level at which decisions are made is related to how quickly changes can be brought in—this is considered below.

Each of these considerations about the knowledge of the planners point to the difficulties in assigning curriculum planning to the national political level. We turn now to further considerations about the appropriate levels of planning for the curriculum, which will further undermine the argument for a national curriculum.

## Levels of decision making

What level of decision making is appropriate to the curriculum? The IPPR, and any other advocate of a compulsory core curriculum, claims that decisions about the curriculum should be made at the national level. The locus of decision making, they argue, should be moved from the sphere of schools to central government. The assumption seems to be that this will not only bring the benefits of national control, but also that there are no costs in changing the locus of control. However, it is crucial to my argument that decision making by government is not costless in this way. When decisions are moved between different levels of decision making, it is not simply the case that a different set of people now make the decisions— the nature of the decision itself can change (Sowell, 1980). In the context of control of the curriculum, the significant issues concern the ease of reversibility of the decision; the possibility of incremental changes; and the ease of fine tuning of the decision.

### *Ease of reversibility*

Consider the discovery of falling standards in reading and the perceived connection between this and the crowding of the primary curriculum with more science, history and geography. If an individual school had experimented with the broadening of its curriculum in this way, then upon discovery of a decline in reading standards, the solution would be obvious and quickly initiated. The headteacher or governors could reverse the previous decision and the next year's intake could then have a more appropriate curriculum. In fact, it is easier than that, because the individual school would not need to await the results of standardised tests administered at the convenience of the central planners: teachers working with pupils would be able to give immediate feedback of problems encountered, and the decision could be reversed well before a whole cohort of pupils had gone through the year. With the experiment conducted at the national level, however, things become extraordinarily complicated, expensive and slow to change. For the curriculum is now on the statute book, brought there by lengthy and slow procedures, and can only be changed via similarly lengthy and slow procedures. We have already witnessed the time it has taken to change the attainment targets and schemes of work in mathematics and science—and perhaps what is most interesting about these changes is how minimalistic and cosmetic they are. Presumably nothing else was possible within the bureaucratic structures.

Moreover, in this example, the feedback mechanism was fairly easily initiated and interpreted. But it is more likely that for feedback about other effects of the national curriculum, the mechanisms will be very hard to put in place, and the time taken between discovering problems and being able to institute a solution will be inordinately long. It will not be until the year 2000 that the current National Curriculum will be fully in place, that is, before the first group of pupils has been taught solely under its regime. But this means that by this time, eleven generations of pupils will have been submitted to the curriculum for some part of their school life. They will have been compelled to follow it, even though an evaluation of its effectiveness could not properly have been made (Kelly, 1990 p. ix).

Even this underestimates the complexity of the problem of feedback. For we have assumed that feedback on the effectiveness of the compulsory curriculum could be obtained by, for example, results in reading tests. Bureaucratic control, of course, needs tangible results such as this by which to monitor whether national goals are being met, and whether the structure of the curriculum needs to be changed. But it is difficult, both in principle and in practice, to suggest what objective and quantifiable measures could be used to ascertain whether *effective education* is taking place. The central planners will need to have some feedback, and hence they are likely to come up with measures which do not really reflect what is important about education. They are likely to dwell on things that can be easily quantified, such as test scores, and truancy rates, rather than on more nebulous aspects of the educational experience. This is not true, of course, of decision makers at school level. They are continually interacting with pupils and aware of the multiplicity of their educational experiences. They are in a much better position to evaluate any changes, even if they are not able to articulate this evaluation to the degree required by state educational administrators.

### Incremental changes and innovation

Second, the change in locus of decision making also changes the ease with which incremental changes can be made; this in turn affects the ease with which innovation can be introduced. Decisions that are reversible are also flexible, allowing for innovations to be introduced and tried out, and perhaps rejected or more widely disseminated. Government-made decisions are much more likely not to foster innovation in this way.

Consider again the reading standards example. If a school discovers this decline then, as noted above, it could quickly reverse the previous decision and eliminate, say, science from the first years of schooling. However, it does not have to do that, it could also make incremental changes—by raising the level of time devoted to science, but not by as much as before. Or it could introduce the innovation of a longer teaching week, allowing more time for science *and* reading. But importantly, these changes could be introduced in a spirit of 'we'll try this and see what happens'. If it is not successful, if reading standards continue to decline, or if children or parents or staff object to the longer hours, then the decisions can again be adjusted until the outcome is as desired. Governments cannot make incremental changes and innovations in this way. Even if the necessary feedback mechanisms could be brought into place, it would be politically inexpedient for governments to persist in introducing incremental changes. The electorate simply would not let them get away with it.

The ability to make innovations is of importance when considering the needs of the economy, as well as of individuals and society. For a state-prescribed curriculum is likely to be in place for decades before significant changes can be made to its content. In our fast-changing world, it seems rather arrogant to suppose that our ideas today of what is technologically, socially and personally appropriate in a curriculum, would be relevant early in the next century.

## Fine-tuning

Finally, another facet of decision-making relationships of relevance to the curriculum relates to the ease with which decisions can be 'fine tuned' to the particular problem at hand. Teachers in schools have continual feedback from their students, and are thus able to assess the effectiveness of the curriculum for *individuals*, and gauge work accordingly. The central planners are clearly not able to fine tune the curriculum to suit the needs of individuals in this way.

One way around this would be to leave the broad framework of the curriculum to the central planners, and allow teachers discretion in the classroom. This is certainly how the IPPR envisages that its curriculum will overcome the types of problems discussed in this section: 'it is essential for teaching to be adapted to the needs and strengths of the learner ... a teacher ... knows the particular circumstances in which learning takes place ... Effective teaching requires the freedom to make specific planning decisions in response to such factors. The national framework should support teachers in such planning, not constrain them unduly' (O'Hear and White, 1991 p. 10). I have already argued why national curricula of the sort envisaged by the IPPR are likely to be highly prescriptive, and not leave areas of the curriculum to the teachers' discretion.

What 'fine tuning' could take place in a curriculum not nationally imposed, in our 'reading versus science' example? Clearly, teachers could encourage those who are able to read to cover areas of science, while allowing those who are not to spend time in mastery of reading. The solution is simple, but the inflexibility of a national curriculum is likely to militate against it. Centrally-imposed decisions are likely to be 'package deals' rather than individualised. Which is more appropriate to the relationship between teacher and pupil?

The considerations of this section, then, lead us further to question whether the appropriate level of decision making for the curriculum is the national one. If the curriculum needs to be flexible, fostering innovation and allowing for incremental changes and 'fine tuning' to cater for the needs of individuals, then national decision making, I have argued, is inappropriate.

Let us be clear how this discussion fits in with the arguments put forward by the IPPR, and other protagonists of a national curriculum. They contend that the national is the appropriate level because of the broader goals already discussed above, including equality of opportunity, and the values of democracy. I have argued in those sections that these goals do not demand a national curriculum. What I have attempted here is to show that there are further issues, which they have not considered, which also undermine the case for central control of the curriculum.

Perhaps the fear of readers who have come with me thus far, is that there is no real alternative. Education in England and Wales was full of problems prior to the introduction of the National Curriculum in 1988. Surely I cannot be suggesting a return to that unpalatable *status quo ante?* I am not. In the closing, perhaps most controversial, section, I shall suggest an alternative.

## THE MARKET ALTERNATIVE

The argument so far has rather negatively concentrated on undermining the arguments *for* a national curriculum. The onus is now on me to suggest how the undeniable problems of state education can be resolved without one. I guess that readers who have followed me this far are likely to balk at my proposals. I have already pointed out how mention of the market tends to raise the hackles of many educationalists. Two things about this. First, I hope the argument of the first four sections will stand on its own, and not depend upon that which follows. Readers might then agree that a national curriculum is undesirable without having to agree with the solution that I propose. Second, the argument given below is a sketch only. There are many issues raised which cannot adequately be covered in the space available—and I have to concentrate on the curriculum, rather than broader issues. I hope it will whet the appetite for more, and provoke discussion: but I do not, of course, expect the arguments as they stand to be convincing on their own. The work for my doctoral thesis would be redundant if that were the case!

Enough of the caveats: I suggest that the alternative is to allow 'internal market forces' to 'control' the curriculum. By 'internal market forces' I do not mean privatising educational provision, selling off schools, instituting fee-paying and so on. I mean simply liberating the demand and the supply sides of education within a *state-provided service*.[2] On the demand side this would involve allowing parental or student choice, or some combination, to express itself, by having 'money follow students'—either through a voucher system or through *per capita* funding—and dropping controls on enrolment. The *supply* side would need to be liberated, to permit a diversity of schools to open, offering a variety of educational experiences with a minimum of regulation, and to be funded in such a way that there is fair competition between these schools—by allowing all schools to be state funded, or to be state subsidised to the same degree.

Clearly, this 'minimum of regulation' will *not* include the demand for a national curriculum, or the compulsory publication of national test results. It may well include inspections of schools.

It is important to note that the 'non-curricula' requirements of the 1988 Education Reform Act, for example, Local Management of Schools, are only first steps towards an internal market in this sense. Crucially, the supply side has not been liberated in the way suggested. It is still very difficult to set up a school, and impossible to 'opt-in' to the state system and receive funding on the same basis as state schools. As I write, this may well be in the process of change, change that would be very welcome indeed.

The mechanism of choice means that parents and students can choose, and move between, schools if the curriculum (in the broadest sense, including the organisation and ethos of the school) is not to their satisfaction. Note, though, that it is not parents and students who *decide* the curriculum. This is still up to professional educationalists—teachers, headteachers, textbook writers, curriculum visionaries. All parents and students decide is whether they approve of the curriculum or not. If they do not, they can vote with their feet (the right of 'exit'), or they can try to influence the curriculum by use of 'voice'—challenging the headteacher or the governors, writing letters to the media, and so on. But the decisions about the curriculum rest completely with the school itself. In this way, the internal market mechanisms lead to a third alternative to those discussed by the IPPR—certainly not *political* control, but not unadulterated *professional* control either. It leads to what might be called *circumscribed professional* control, professional control with checks and balances.

Many doubts, I suspect, will have occurred to the reader already. I shall consider four principal objections. Is it not the case, first, that the internal market mechanisms will allow a 'privileged group' to decide the curriculum, when it should be decided by all? Second, that these mechanisms will create curriculum chaos? Third, that a 'lowest common denominator' curriculum will emerge, neglecting higher pursuits?

Finally, that a market needs a national curriculum, to provide information to the customers?


## *'Privileged' groups*

Why should parents, students and educationalists be given the right to 'control' the curriculum in this way, when issues about the curriculum affect everyone in society? Should not the political implications of the curriculum mean that the polity as a whole should decide on its content? This objection has already been discussed under the section on democratic control of the curriculum above. There it was pointed out that there was no necessary link between something having political implications and the need for political control, that it was contingent factors which would point to the need for political control. I am suggesting that these contingent factors show that the time is ripe for 'circumscribed professional' control.


## *Order without design?*

The IPPR labelled schooling without a national curriculum a 'hit-and-miss' affair (O'Hear and White, 1991 p. 5), and this is a common reaction against the notion of involving any market mechanisms in education: Andy Green, for example, lambasts the notion with the phrases 'chaotic', 'obdurately fragmented', 'unsystematic', 'untidy', and 'a kind of British muddle' (Green, 1991).

So would this internal market control of the curriculum lead to chaos? I do not see why at all. First, we do have evidence of market control of the curriculum, in the private sectors in this country, the USA and Japan. In Britain, there is no political control of the curriculum in private schools, but what is found could be described as a *de facto*, but *flexible* national curriculum. The majority of private schools offer a similar core of academic subjects, together with some vocational elements. The diversity usually emerges on the fringes—some schools specialising in drama, dance, and so on, others in further academic pursuits, or others still in the ethos and organisation of the school. There is no compulsion which has made this the case—order has emerged without design. In this context, we can refer back to the suggestion that the curriculum up to 1904 in England and Wales arose in exactly this way—no central authority designing it, but order nonetheless.

Second, further support for the plausibility of order arising without design can be obtained from the following 'thought experiment': suppose there is a market in education, with the curriculum unregulated, and we wish to set up a school. It is 1992. What should we include in the school curriculum? Are there any constraints on us? Clearly, there are. If we offered a curriculum of Bingo, Learning Telephone Pages and Ndebele, we would not get many takers, so would be forced to close. Even if a few very ignorant or frivolous parents chose our school, perhaps because it was nearby, or they liked the glossy brochure, then it is unlikely that there would be enough of them to make it worthwhile for us to continue. (This relates to the general point that not everyone has to be informed for the market to work, as long as some are.) So we offer what parents and children want—a core of English, maths and science, together with a smattering of humanities and the arts, vocational subjects and physical education. We would, however, be able to throw in something extra if we wanted to. This could be anything that we felt was educationally important, from drama to slanting the content of the curriculum to a multicultural focus. Or we could offer something distinctive about the ethos or organisation of the school. We are definitely constrained, but within those constraints we can be flexible and innovative.

Now suppose it is 1692. We are setting up an educational establishment for gentlemen, probably private tuition. Again, we would be constrained to work within the cultural context, and offer the appropriate curriculum. Perhaps we would use Henry Peacham's *Compleat Gentleman* of 1622 and offer history, cosmography, geometry, poetry, music, drawing and painting in oil, heraldry, exercises of the body and fishing (Watson, 1909 p. 98), Or we could use any number of other similar texts as a basis for our curriculum. Again, we might offer certain innovations corresponding to our pet interests. But nothing too radical, or we would not be offered employment.

Finally, suppose we are setting up school in 2022, say. What would we put on the curriculum then? If the current National Curriculum had had a good innings, I suggest we would offer something rather similar to that—but I doubt very much if it would be relevant to the society that had evolved by that time. But suppose there had been a market-led curriculum for some time. Then I refuse to predict what we would offer. But I suggest that we would very easily pick up what was desired by our 'customers'. There would be a core curriculum clearly apparent in the educational establishments around, and it would be to this that we would relate our curriculum.

Order can be divorced from design. There does not have to be chaos without government intervention.

## A 'fast food' education?

Will not popular control of the curriculum bring about a 'lowest common denominator', a 'fast food' education for the masses? This objection could run in one of two, mutually opposed, ways (which says something rather interesting about perceptions of the market, I think). First, it could be objected that a popular curriculum would be a completely undemanding one, with schools fulfilling little more than a 'child-minding' function. Interestingly enough, an American company is about to embark on building a chain of low-cost, popular schools across the US, definitely the 'MacDonald's of private education' (*Daily Telegraph*, 27 May 1992). The company is doing its market research, and is finding that what parents and students want is precisely not the undemanding education suggested above, but a curriculum based on academic and vocational subjects, and firm on discipline. I suggest that the evidence of what private schools offer in this country, too, points to such a curriculum being offered—for private education is not now the province of only one particular class. Moreover, it is the opposite objection that came from 'the right' in the 1970s, that parents and students wanted demanding subjects, but it was the 'trendy' educationalists who foisted a watered-down curriculum upon them.

But just suppose there were some parents or students who were attracted to an undemanding curriculum, say of playing fruit machines all day. After all, Summerhill has been criticised for appealing to some children in precisely that way. We come back to the point reiterated several times throughout this paper, that if this was the case (and I claim it would be highly unlikely), then a specific solution to this specific problem would be what was required. The internal market does not rule out inspections of schools. If these found the curriculum to be unsatisfactory—and the school could not demonstrate in what ways it was satisfactory—then corresponding action could be taken. This is exactly the situation now when parents decide to educate their children at home. Again, this would not require a national curriculum to compare and assess the curriculum on offer. All that would be needed was for the inspectorate to be aware of *rules of thumb*, connected with what was generally accepted to be part of a good education. One rule of thumb would no doubt be not to let children sit around all day playing fruit machines, unless it could be clearly demonstrated that this fitted in with some wider ethos of the school—that it was part of children's development, say, to becoming autonomous in their educational pursuits.

The opposing objection to this then might be that popular education would be bad precisely because it would reflect deeply conservative attitudes towards education. Popular education would stress discipline and academic subjects and not progressive ideals. I think there is something in this—but it brings us back to a crucial notion. The internal market that I am defending offers *professional control of the curriculum, with checks and balances.* It is not that the customers will suddenly become all-powerful. The professional educationalists will still be there, with their interests and predilections. Teachers will be imbued with their educational traditions and cultures, and with ideals about what makes up a good education. It will still be up to them to establish the curriculum on offer. If there is a clash of interests between these and what the masses want from their education, there will no doubt be compromises, and a process of evolution and experimentation. But notice that those who would offer this objection assume that the educationalists are correct in opposing the supposed conservative ideals of the populace. I do not want to make that assumption. Ordinary people may well be in a very good position to know what they want from their schooling. It is worth remembering that in the 1870s ordinary people wanted their children to learn literacy and numeracy, in a cosy nearby room; the educational reformers forced them into cold, regimented classrooms and compelled them to learn religion and factory discipline. Perhaps the fads and fancies of our current educational establishment will seem as arcane in years to come. They might not, but it is up to the educationalists to convince the people that their ideas are worth adhering to. But it seems supinely arrogant for educational experts to feel they can simply impose their will on the people, without having to win over their 'intellects and dispositions' in the give-and-take of the internal market-place.

*Does the internal market need a national curriculum?*

Finally, it has been contended by some that an internal market needs a national curriculum. For example, Clyde Chitty argues that informed parent choice requires a national curriculum: 'the [National] Curriculum does, after all, act as justification for a massive programme of national testing at 7, 11, 14 and 16 which will, in turn, provide evidence to parents for the desirability or otherwise of individual schools'

(Chitty, 1989 p. 218). Markets can only work effectively, he argues, if there is 'maximum consumer information'.

I suggest that Chitty has here too literally applied the neo-classical theory of perfect competition. In a perfectly competitive market it is true that perfect knowledge is needed. But perfectly competitive markets do not exist in the real world, they are—to the neo-classical economists—simply a useful model on which to make predictions. In a perfectly competitive education market, schools would need to supply consumers with perfect information. Chitty is saying that such information could come from national testing. But we know (and of course he knows) that it is not possible to have totally reliable and valid tests, nor would it be possible to analyse the results in a way that truly reflected the 'value added' by the school. Moreover, even if it was, not many would want to argue that such tests truly reflected all of what was educationally valuable in schools. So what we are left with is that the information from national testing is at best very imperfect and, at worst, positively misleading (because of unreliability, invalidity, and no accurate means of presenting the value added). Given these imperfections, we are left with the notion that for the imperfect market of educational provision, the consumers need information, true, but that, as in any other imperfect market, this information can be acquired through various imperfect mechanisms. National testing derived from a national curriculum could be one of these, but because of its expense and inconvenience is unlikely to be rated highly compared with other measures. These could include considerations of a school's informal reputation, observations of pupils in the school and in the neighbourhood, subjective evaluations about the appearance of the school, discipline, reputation, etc. It may be that consumer organisations would come up with exam results as being of importance, and they might publish statistical sample surveys of schools, even conduct standardised tests. But to suppose that, just because there is a market, this requires standardised *national* testing, is to seriously misunderstand the nature of the market.

A second argument for the market's need of a national curriculum rests on a similar confusion. The suggestion is that the market needs the product or service on offer to be 'the same everywhere' (Bash and Coulby, 1989 p. 19-20). But this is again taking the neo-classical economists' criteria for there to be a perfectly competitive market too seriously. A competing conception of the market, offered by Hayek, is that product differentiation and diversity are the hallmarks of the dynamics of competition. If this approach is accepted (and I find it persuasive), then we can reject the notion that competition in the market needs a national curriculum.

Neither of these arguments for a national curriculum hold. The internal market does not need a national curriculum in order to function properly. Moreover, the arguments in this section suggest that the principal objections to allowing the internal market to 'control' the curriculum are unfounded. The 'privileged group' argument would only be relevant if it had been established that political control of the curriculum was desirable—which has not been established. The market mechanisms were shown to be capable of creating an ordered but flexible curriculum, not chaos. Neither challenge to the 'fast-food' curriculum emerged unscathed.

It is now necessary to draw all the threads of the argument together. I have argued against the case for a national curriculum. I have put forward an alternative, and suggested that it could overcome certain objections. But the important issue remains of whether these market mechanisms could tackle the problems with state education encountered earlier. Moreover, could they satisfy the aspirations of the philosophers? These issues will now be addressed in the concluding section.

## BREAKING THE CODE

The Napoleonic Code of 1804 laid the foundations for a national curriculum throughout France. In 1988, an unlikely British Napoleon, Kenneth Baker, instituted the same for England and Wales. My aim in this paper has been to undermine the case for such a 'code' to be imposed on education in this country.

In the first sections, I countered each of the arguments in favour of a national curriculum. It was not the case, I argued, that a national curriculum could raise standards, nor could it help promote equality of opportunity. What was needed for both was improved teaching techniques, and targeted resources. Continuity between schools and curriculum coherence were again matters of teachers' awareness rather than a compulsory curriculum. The specific issues of 'sink' and 'problem' schools needed specific solutions, not a national curriculum for all schools, problematic or not. Moreover, economic competitiveness would be unlikely to be enhanced by the rigidity of an inflexible national curriculum.

As far as the philosophical arguments went, democratic control of the curriculum was seen to be desirable only in a much better—perhaps impossible to achieve—democracy. Education for participation in democracy taken seriously would lead to a cumbersome, over-prescriptive curriculum, that would alienate students and teachers alike. It seemed undesirable to overburden the school curriculum with 'education for autonomy', when the school was just one of many institutions already functioning to instil the requisite qualities, especially as this could act to undermine the effectiveness of these other institutions.

Having looked at some of the concerns raised by a centralised curriculum, the knowledge of the curriculum planners, and the appropriate levels of decision making about education, I then pointed to an alternative, leaving curriculum 'control' to the internal market. I tackled several objections to such control, but I have not yet established why I see the internal market as overcoming any of the problems of state education, or as fitting in with the aspirations of the philosophers. I shall now turn to these issues.

My two basic contentions are that the internal market will act as a check and balance on the teaching profession, to ensure it is 'kept up to scratch'; and second that it will not divert resources into unnecessary bureaucracy. These have implications for each of the problems raised about state education prior to the National Curriculum. With checks and balances on the teaching profession, it will be much harder for weaker teachers to get away with providing a curriculum for children which is inappropriate, or which overlaps what they have been taught already in other schools, or which does not challenge them. Of course it will not stop these things altogether—but a national curriculum can not go any way to solving these problems. Crucially, not all parents and students have to be informed or concerned with the market for teachers to be 'kept on their toes' in this way. Similarly, the market mechanisms can provide additional insurance—as was previously noted—against schools becoming 'sink' or 'problem' schools. Market signals, of reduced income, will be sent to the school management if the curriculum is failing to satisfy parents and students, to prompt them into appropriate action. These signals may be enough. If they are not, then specific government action, through the inspectorate, can be focused on these schools. This brings us to the important issue that, for equality of opportunity, what is needed is for additional resources to be directed at children in need, not diffused throughout the community. Leaving curriculum decisions to schools releases the massive sums of money now being appropriated by the central curriculum planners, allowing these resources to be directed where they are needed. The internal market in the curriculum could enhance equality of opportunity in this way.

Now, what about the aspirations of the philosophers—surely the internal market can not satisfy those? I suggest that it can. One motivation for democratic control is the need for the accountability of particular interest groups such as teachers. The internal market brings in checks and balances to control the teaching profession. It makes the profession accountable, not it is true to *everyone*, but that, as we have noted, is something of a chimera. It does make the profession accountable to all those who use the service, which I suggest is far more preferable.

Finally, even in relation to the IPPR's favoured notion of autonomy, the internal market scores highly. For we have seen that a national curriculum for autonomy confined to schools (and anything else would be on the slippery slope to totalitarianism) could well undermine other institutions which are already geared to promoting some of the desired qualities. The internal market can act to strengthen these other institutions, by giving scope for the self determination of parents and children about educational matters. Choosing schools can itself be an educative process.

Baker's educational *Code Napoleon* is a travesty of a curriculum, imposing a tired image of the 'good old days' of 1904, at great expense, and great inconvenience, onto the teaching profession. But the alternative Code of the IPPR, could be just as bad: a cumbersome, over-prescriptive and costly mechanism, burdening teachers, and diverting resources away from those in genuine need. Let us break the code, focus attention on those who are in need, and entrust to the internal market provision for those who are not.

## FOOTNOTES

1   Notwithstanding difficulties defining its geographical boundaries: compare White, 1990 p. 145 with O'Hear and White, 1991 p. 10, also see White, 1990 pp. 170-1.
2   Actually, I am moderating my usual argument for the purposes of this monograph. Sometimes I do argue for a much greater role for 'market forces', and a removal altogether of state provision in education. But nothing here hinges on such radical suggestions.

## REFERENCES


Aldrich, R. (1992) Educational legislation of the 1980s in England: an historical analysis, *History of Education* 1992 21(1) 57-69

Ball, S. J. (1990) *Politics and Policy Making in Education: Explorations in Policy Sociology.* London: Routledge.

Bash, L. and Coulby, D. (1989) *The Education Reform Act: Competition and Control.* London: Cassell Education.

Cato, V. and Whetton, C. (1991) *An Enquiry into Local Education Authority Evidence on Standards of Reading of Seven-Year Old Children.* London: Department of Education and Science.

Chitty, C. (1989) *Towards a New Education System: The Victory of the New Right?* Lewes: Falmer Press.

Chubb, J. E. and Moe, T. M. (1990) *Politics, Markets and America's Schools.* Washington DC: The Brookings Institution.

Cox, C. B. and Dyson, A. E. (eds.) (1969) *Fight for Education: A Black Paper.* Manchester: Critical Quarterly Association.

Crick, B. and Porter, A. (1978) *Political Education and Political Literacy.* London: Longman.

Dearden, R. F. (1980) Education and Politics, *Journal of Philosophy of Education* 14(2) 149-146.

Department of Education and Science and Welsh Office (1987) *The National Curriculum 5-16: A Consultation Document.* London: HMSO.

Department of Education and Science (1989) *National Curriculum: From Policy to Practice.* London: HMSO.

Department of Education and Science (1991) *Appropriation Accounts 1990-91: Vol 8 Classes XI and XII: Education and Science and Arts and Libraries.* London: HMSO 16 October.

Green, A. (1991), The structure of the system: proposals for change, in Chitty, Clyde (ed.) (1991) *Changing the Future: Redprint for Education.* London: the Tufnell Press.

Green, D. (1985) *Working-class Patients and the Medical Establishment.* Aldershot: Temple Smith (Gower).

Hayek, F. A. (1960) *The Constitution of Liberty*. London: Routledge.

Hirst, P. H. (1992) Education, Knowledge and Practices, in *Papers of the 26th Annual Conference*, Philosophy of Education Society of Great Britain, 24-26 April.

Kelly, A. V. (1990) *The National Curriculum: A Critical Review*. London: Paul Chapman Publishing.

Kirk, G. (1986) *The Core Curriculum*. Sevenoaks: Hodder and Stoughton Educational.

McLean, M. (1990) *Britain and a Single Market Europe*. London: Kogan Page.

Mason, K. and Tooley, J. (1992) *Moving Forward in Mathematics: A Diagnostic Teaching Approach*, (Three volumes). Windsor: NFER-Nelson.

Matthews, K. and Benjamin, D. (1992) *US and UK Unemployment Between the Wars: A Doleful Story*. London: Institute of Economic Affairs.

Murray, C. (1984) *Losing Ground: American Social Policy, 1950-1980*. New York: Basic Books.

National Curriculum Council (1990) *The National Curriculum Council Corporate Plan 1990-91*, February. York: National Curriculum Council.

National Curriculum Council (1991) *Report on Monitoring the Implementation of the National Curriculum Core Subjects 1989-90*. York: National Curriculum Council.

Oakeshott, M. (1962) *Rationalism in Politics and Other Essays*. London: Methuen.

O'Hear, P. and White, J. (1991) *A National Curriculum for All: Laying the Foundations for Success*. London: Institute for Public Policy Research.

Polanyi, M. (1958) *Personal Knowledge*. London: Routledge & Kegan Paul.

Riker, W (1982) *Liberalism Against Populism*. San Francisco: W H Freeman.

Secondary Examinations and Assessment Council (1991) *The Secondary Examinations and Assessment Council Corporate Plan 1991-4*, April. London: SEAC.

Sowell, T. (1980) *Knowledge and Decisions*. New York: Basic Books.

Sowell, T. (1990) *Preferential Policies: An International Perspective*. New York: William Morrow and Company.

Tooley, J. (1990) Education Adequate for Participation in a Democracy, *Papers of the Annual Conference*, Philosophy of Education Society of Great Britain, 20-22 April.

Tooley, J. (1991) Social Choice Theory and Philosophy of Education, *Papers of the Celebration Conference*, Philosophy of Education Society of Great Britain, April.

Watson, F. (1909) *The Beginnings of the Teaching of Modern Subjects in England*. London: Sir Isaac Pitman & Sons.

West, E. G. (1970) *Education and the State*. London: Institute of Economic Affairs, 2nd edition.

White, J. (1973) *Towards a Compulsory Curriculum*. London: Routledge & Kegan Paul.

White, J. (1981) In Defence of State-Controlled Curricula, *Journal of Philosophy of Education* 15(2) 255-260.

White, J. (1988) Two National Curricula: Baker's and Stalin's. Towards a Liberal Alternative, *British Journal of Educational Studies*, 36(3) 218-231.

White, J. (1990) *Education and the Good Life*. London: Kogan Page.

## Changing literacies: Media education and modern culture
### David Buckingham

'TV zombies', 'witless media dupes' or techno-whiz-kids? What will changing media technologies make of our children? David Buckingham argues that the proposal to remove media education from the National Curriculum for English ignores the central importance of the media in children's lives and the rise of new forms of technologically inspired literacy. The children in our schools today must inhabit the media-oriented, technical, cultural and literary landscape of the twenty-first century. We must not shrink from providing them with the competence and understanding which will enable them to inhabit this landscape with ease.
*ISBN 1 872767 61 3      28 pp    paperback        £3.95*


## Partnership in teacher training: Talk and chalk
### Clare Hake

Learning on the job will not produce teachers who can reflect on, compare, and thereby improve their practice. Clare Hake applauds the recent shift in emphasis towards more school-based teacher training, but argues that university departments of education can and must make a continuing contribution to training. In the space created by a partnership between school and college, students can conduct 'an active and rational exploration of the task of teaching'. Using her own experience first as a mentor for trainee teachers in school, and later as a university curriculum tutor, Clare Hake describes and illustrates the advantages of the partnership between school and college exemplified by the Oxford University teacher training scheme. School experience may be paramount but impoverished without the opportunity for reflection provided by such a partnership.
*ISBN 1 872767 46 X      36 pp   paperback        £3.95*


## Education and the crisis in values: should we be philosophical about it?
### Graham Haydon

'Education should seek to impart moral values'—what does this mean? *Does* society face a moral crisis? Does the increasingly public expression of a plurality of moral values signal a decline or an advance? Can education help us with the plurality of values with which we have to live? Graham Haydon addresses these complex issues, arguing that philosophy *can* both help us to understand the current crisis in values and to deal with it. While philosophy may not provide teachers with a lifeline for survival in the classroom, philosophers just might prove to be swimming instructors. Philosophy need not be remote from popular understanding, and should be brought more fully into the training of teachers and into the curriculum of our children to provide this necessary support
*ISBN 1 872767 56 7      25 pp    paperback        £3.95*

### The aims of school history: The National Curriculum and beyond
Peter Lee, John Slater, Paddy Walsh and John White with a preface by
Denis Shemilt

Why is it important to include history in the school curriculum? Is it because the subject (and its methodology) is so profoundly educative that it can be engaged in for its own sake? Or should the study of the past be harnessed to purposes such as preparation for democratic citizenship? These and other questions highlighted by the introduction of the National Curriculum are discussed here by historians and philosophers. The result is a lively and stimulating debate that has important implications for the future of school history.
*ISBN 1 872767 26 5      55 pp    paperback            £4.50*

### Time to change the 1981 Education Act
Brahm Norwich

Brahm Norwich reviews the workings of the 1981 Education Act and how far the special education provision it was intended to enhance has been affected by the 1988 Education Act and subsequent developments. He argues for a reassessment of the definition of special educational need and for tightening the link between assessment of need and provision. Concern for the protection of provision on changing circumstances also prompts him to recommend that duties placed on local education authorities by the 1981 Act should be now extended to school governing bodies, and that parents should have the choice of a quicker form of decision making.
*ISBN 1 872767 36 2      36 pp   paperback            £3.95*

### The promise and perils of educational comparison
Martin McLean

Can Britain's relatively poor economic performance be blamed on its inferior schools and teaching? Politicians in recent years have increasingly supported their proposals for educational reform with examples of practice in other countries. Against this background Martin McLean examines the uses and possible abuses of the discipline of comparative education. He illustrates his argument with many possible examples, concluding that the challenge to those who turn to other systems of education to find support for their arguments is whether they can let their thinking 'take in deeper and wider perspectives and whether they can accept the conclusions that emerge'.
*ISBN 1 872767 31 1      40 pp   paperback            £3.95*

### National Curriculum science: So near and yet so far
Arthur Jennings

When the first proposals for the National Curriculum science were published in 1988 the goal of giving all pupils a broad and exciting experience of science seemed to be within reach. Arthur Jennings traces here the history of implementation and asks whether, under pressure of accommodating a workable system of assessment, that original goal has not been lost. Teachers will need to be vigilant, he urges, and carry parents and school governors with them, if they are to go beyond teaching 'to the tests' and achieve a real experience of science for all.
*ISBN 1 872767 41 9      41 pp   paperback            £3.95*

## The arts 5-16: Changing the agenda
### John White

John White critically examines the central issues that underlie the National Curriculum Council's document *The Arts 5-16: A curriculum framework*. Education in the arts has lacked a coherent sense of purpose and whilst the NCC has tried to provide an integrated policy it has paid insufficient attention to the underlying aims of education in the arts. In addressing this problem John White presents a searching discussion of the purposes and underlying assumptions of education in the arts and their practical realisation. His concern is to ensure that the foundations for work in school in the arts are secure and defensible and above all will generate a love of art.

*ISBN 1 872767 06 0     38 pp     paperback          £3.95*

## More has meant women: the feminisation of schooling
### Jane Miller

'To an extent that is quite inadequately recognised, state education is provided by women; as is virtually all schooling, whether public or private, for young children.' Jane Miller argues that criticism of current educational practice often has gender as its hidden target. She draws on historical evidence and on her own teaching experience to develop a complex and provocative discussion.

*ISBN 1 872767 21 4     31 pp     paperback          £3.95*

## Music education and the National Curriculum
### Keith Swanwick

Keith Swanwick discusses the evolution of music education in schools and critically examines the implications of the attainment targets in the National Curriculum. On the central question of music as knowledge he considers that the National Curriculum Working Group put a misplaced emphasis on factual information and quantity. Knowing about and understanding music is much more than processing factual information and any form of assessment must recognise *qualitative* awareness rather than acquisition of *quantitative* facts. Swanwick's improved criteria for assessment have in part been accepted by the Secretary of State for Education. In this strongly argued work Swanwick seeks to identify a way forward for music in the classroom that would secure the confidence of musicians and music educators.

*ISBN 1 872767 11 7     33 pp     paperback          £3.95*

*the Tufnell Press*
*47 Dalmeny Road,*
*London, N7 0DY*

## ORDER FORM

Please send me the following:

|  | Price | Quantity | Total |
|---|---|---|---|
|  |  |  |  |
|  |  |  |  |
|  |  |  |  |
|  |  |  |  |
|  |  |  |  |
|  |  |  |  |
|  |  |  |  |

Total amount enclosed

## Please make cheques payable to the Tufnell Press

NAME _______________________________

ADDRESS _______________________________

_______________________________

_______________________________

IN10/1993